As
If

Books by James Richardson

Reservations
Second Guesses
As If
How Things Are
Vectors: Aphorisms and Ten-Second Essays
Interglacial: New and Selected Poems and Aphorisms
By the Numbers: Poems and Aphorisms
During
For Now

Thomas Hardy: The Poetry of Necessity
Vanishing Lives: Style and Self in Tennyson,
    D. G. Rossetti, Swinburne and Yeats

As If

JAMES RICHARDSON

Carnegie Mellon University Press
Pittsburgh 2023

Cover design by Jess Jones

Library of Congress Control Number 2023933207
ISBN 978-0-88748-697-5
Copyright © 1992 by James Richardson
Printed and bound in the United States of America

10 9 8 7 6 5 4 3 2 1

As If was selected for the National Poetry Series by Amy Clampitt and was first published by Persea Books, New York, New York in 1992.

First Carnegie Mellon University Press Classic Contemporaries Edition, October 2023.

CONTENTS

I TO AUTUMN

Anyway   11
In Fog   12
Splinters   13
Fruit Flies   14
Two Rumors   15
Blue Heron, Winter Thunder   17
To Autumn   19
For Now   21
How It Ends   23

II SHORT CUTS

Signs, Signs!   27
The Given   28
The Mind-Body Problem   29
Locusts   30
My Mistake   31
Cat Among Stones   32
Henry   33
Post-Romantic   34
The Pitch   35
Sand   36
Men in Tuxes   37
Last Autumn   38
In Our Elements   39
A Pause   41
Askance and Strangely   42
A Measure   43

III CHILDREN'S CHILDREN

Out of School   47
Early Violets   49
Where I Live   50
Settlers   53

Marigolds   55
Song for Kate   56
At First, At Last   61
For the Children   74
Elegy for Either of Us   77
As If Ending   78

for Kate and L.C., first
for Julie and Ted, my teachers
for Connie, after all

I

TO AUTUMN

ANYWAY

The way an acre of starlings towers and pours
rapidly through itself, a slipping knot,
landing so few feet down the furrows (the whole skywriting
like a secret no one knows they have given away)
is one of those breathtaking wastes
(sun and the seeds they feed on being others)
in which something senseless, even selfish, absurdly magnified,
becomes grandeur (love is another).
Sometimes the flock, banking in unison,
vanishes an instant, like a sheet of paper edge-on
(a secret, anyway, is the illusion
confessing it would make a difference).
I watched this happen once—two seconds, hours—
till I understood no kindness, not a shadow or stone.
And they did not come back,
though I waited all evening (and it was you
I waited for). Though the sky turned black.

IN FOG

Sometimes, early and cold, you stumble
into the land's confusion
of tract and interstate with cracked harrow
and with fog, and with fog again.

The meadows, deepening, go stoneless.
Head-on two cars,
in a blaze, transpose.
There is nothing that is not everywhere.

And the jet extending through the fog like fog,
surrounding drone,
and the trill arriving as a blur
of any bird or other than bird,

and the houses, fogbound, that digress
in vague contrition,
smoking upward, flooding the road:
you take them in with a breath.

And breathe out feather, rock, and engine,
lightly, lightly, for the fog avers
that to forget and begin again
is not different from going on and on.

Just by looking, or not looking too hard,
you can love anything, says the fog.
You can gaze straight into the sun,
grayed and mild, now, as a moon.

Shrewd is unkind, I chose nothing, it sighs
louder and louder as the day
takes hold, and all the years,
and that it was wrong becomes clearer and clearer.

SPLINTERS

They must have streamed like thistledown
from that first deep splinter,
surfacing in the scar, and yearly
further up my side, and fainter.

I thought I could feel them, childishly,
school along my heart, or rise
as starlings shearing in crosswinds
of November, my inner land.

A failing cry in the clouds, the tremor
of the frost-iris ringing the moon
may be night migration, or their slide,
translucent, over the mind's eye.

In the flush, the tenderness, the shying,
suddenly something, microscopic—
lost, often, in the tweezing,
so I wonder *Was that it, was there anything?*

If they are new ones, as I am told,
I never remember getting them,
though I think often in this season
of lengthening walks *On this path here,*

or there, I must have. When love alters,
for all your watching, isn't it sudden,
though no matter where you look,
or how far back, you find and find the reason?

FRUIT FLIES

Though you cellar it in the shrewdest cold,
airtight, and without the faintest print
or contusion, thinking of nothing,
and lounge at sundown by a golden window,
they will descend, as if remembering,
on whatever is turning.

You will hear in a drowse their breezeless
pervasion of your screens all evening
and not know whether darkness
or a hand-size swarm of them conspires
to disturb, in your hand, the focus of a pear.

And then, because your noticing makes more,
they are everywhere, a graininess in vision,
as if you had stayed up past your usual hour,
or some memory had persisted all year
as hands near your hand, an air on the air.

What you have spared all year, unwillingly,
they love to the stone, a live annihilation,
and when nothing is left whole they settle,
uncloyed, over your spills, or concentrate
in a clouded spoon.
              Or shade, when your eyes must close,
your moist lids, or the little bridge of your lips,
and behind your ear the finger of cologne,
and everywhere you open, the sweet fluids.
                            So close at last
you cannot say where the delve and pause
of your breathing ends, and they begin,
something like passion, only helpless and weary,
something like darkness, only rife and wild,
body that fills your body to the eyes.

TWO RUMORS

1   *As a Ghost*

Somehow in a November fever
to see you once more as you were
before our life—no bitterness
of mine taken into your face—
I was a ghost, all eyes
as you hastened from room to room
or, reading under a narrow light,
muttered to yourself, alone.
What came over you
was my breathing, like an untouched glass,
loss, my alcohol.

Something silken and unshy
that you might draw, pointing your foot,
up the sheer of your calf and thigh,
I rose on you, I rounded you
with water's faint
lift of your breasts, with the wind's lift,
spreading your hair.

And I was lost forever
unless I could remember,
as a ghost, and faithless,
what I had to remember
before your mind changed, or the windows grayed,
or the phone rang and I heard you speak of me.

2   *As a Lake*

Now I am vastness, and gone, I mourn
nothing under the broad, pale sun.
How my springs enter, cool or sour,
consumes me, and the glint and drive
of the many bodies of my body
are miles. Now I am calm,
towering and calm, I learn
how the sky fathomed us, so small
it could not say we were two,
or where we were.

What you believed, I heard,
and what remained of us, I endured,
though what came over me
now, as a lake, I know
was the stress of a leaf, a riding cloud.

BLUE HERON, WINTER THUNDER

All up and down the coast that November,
driving or reading, I heard it, over my shoulder,
tinnier than summer's, winter thunder.
Was it the first ever or, disbelieving,
had I forgotten the sound, resounding stone,
that hollowed me, that caught me rising—
brief shame, a truck of wind, a clearing?

Every evening, bridging the horizons,
one of those hours-long clouds, oily and bronze,
that as a child . . . that I still think are great fish—
or thoughts I cannot have for decades yet—
cruised over, soundless, or larger than hearing,
or in the astonishment of congratulation,
and I breathed thickly, safe at my depth.

We looked up, always, into the sourceless brightness
of like becoming more like, of days blending together.
One dawn, or every one, leaves broke into our room
with a strange slowness, a live glow.
Once or a thousand times we turned
sideways, passing in the narrow hall,
and you repeated: what was so true I won't remember.

How many times was it April? Rod in a soft arch,
I dragged my lure repeatedly over drowned brush
where I felt, as if it were in me down in the darkness,
the tremble, the soft mouth, nearly a strike,
though I was surely worrying the bottom.
How provocative hope is, how querulous!
And here is another thing I cannot say slowly enough.

How, when my gaze stood hard on the sky,
a cloud slipped, spring broke, the lake opened—
no the lake *had* opened, cryless,
and there was mountainous invisibility, or wings

blue-gray at first, then lucid: sky before I could point.
And I *did* point, though I was alone.
Or: where I pointed, wings rose, I was alone.

Thunderously. But was there thunder,
staggering the day, and did November
show for an instant through that shaken April,
chill, dark rising, then for a moment, stars?
Blue heron, the books said. Habits, ordinary.
Wingspread? Miles less than in imagination.
No thunder, I read and read. No consolation.

November, the jet blew up on our slope and burned.
That's what the papers said, that's what I must have seen.
But when God asks: I heard the crash first and saw—
as if I'd been pouring gas that backflashed—
the plane, still high, already on fire
with the future. I turned and there was no one there.
I turned, and there was no one there for years.

I still look up. The furnace ignites, rumbling,
in the blue, early dark. A blow of leaves.
Not swiftly, *suddenly* that heron vanishes—
as if offscreen. The flash not lightning,
the long resounding *longer* of no thunder.
Because you are out of time
you shall wake again and again and not remember.

As if your face, our story, as if day after day
were the sheen in someone's hair. Shift, not there.
And, sky darkening, I looked past my reflection
down into turbid waters, phosphorescent limbs,
pleasure to water, pain to dark water,
and there was the night, or the day in negative:
among the slim white trunks, white rain, white rain.

TO AUTUMN

As orange as you could want it, oranger,
someone's "Last Leaf" or the sun-daub of a child,
it teeters on the guardrail, that disembodied van,
doors swanned, windshield blown,
the driver, I want to think, astonished
in his last image, hurtling on and on.

Gone or gone ahead?—the wind's question,
rising as if to follow him, expires
with the geese in rippling formations,
not V's, but the tide's graphs of wrack and litter,
and with enough complaint in their heavy rowing
that you know what a steep thin stair it is they climb.

We've been listening on and off to their sounding
of a day so fiery and steep, of such transparency
it could be thirty autumns—maple consumed with maple,
hills that fade and plead within red hills
as in embers, or the view, behind closed lids,
of the red, the rose-black fathoms of the body.

There's a story in one of my lost childhood books
that's been changing since I left it out in the rain
where a girl's yearning at the water's rim
draws sixty geese along the Atlantic flyway,
and whether she made, summoned, or deeply entered them,
at the touch of a southern pond, they turn human.

Hardly knowing curse from blessing,
they stood, earth-shaken, unremembering,
and their gaunt bodies flourished and divided,
hugely smooth, to the heart, and what they saw
first in their giant clarity was that all
they had overflown, map-height, was insurmountable.

If I could be sure nothing was worth that pain,
I would wake forever from the dream I wake to,
not a lit window, not a sound in range:
that I am caught, world failing, in the speed of my mind
and could read a novel between your breaths or watch,
on the silent turnpike, traffic frozen in lanes.

I cannot wake you, I must never speak,
since a touch would welt your brow, and even a whisper
strike, at this speed, loud enough to kill.
They also, gazing down at the water's mirror,
saw through the planet into the other sky,
and not a creature they could imagine could bear desire.

Winds in my ears contending, thirty landings
knee-deep in a planet deeper and bluer than wind,
if I could look up your look would say *Stranger,*
a man's rage at his life, when all is said,
is a rage to be more deeply deceived.
How you walk so slow and keep up is the mystery.

The geese, hitting a level, swerve and re-descend.
They need no South. Suburbia's awash with feed.
The office ponds are warm, and as for poisons,
it takes more than one life to be sure what's killing you.
There's something about staying in exactly the same place
that's so much like continuously leaving.

I see in the downcast lake's revolving: *Fire!*
—that is the flicker of your coat, or brakelights
as someone hurtles through a windshield to a window
and becomes the everywhere of November sky
looking back for us, the wind his disregard
aloud, those geese the scatter of his eyes.

FOR NOW

The doorless barn holds nothing
out or in.
What you hear, if you listen,
is your listening.

Motionless the pruned limb,
half way down,
the heat of the blade still on it,
the resinous tang.

Soundlessly a swallow's
contained fright
crosses a sill forever,
part dark, part in light,

though the urgent stone,
which the spell allows
to hang like a small gray moon,
forgets to follow,

and the storming child is absorbed,
mid-leap, mid-fall,
whether in rage or remorse
you cannot tell.

Fantastic, lengthened out,
his cry or call,
like a record winding down,
has deepened, inaudible.

Would they hear it, if they turned,
those lovers, turning,
on the point of a declaration,
coming or going?

All morning for a cheek to warm,
an hour to unclose an eye.
Is it joy, is it pain that lingers,
or surprise

at the stillness spreading in rings
from their last words,
endlessly *For now,*
whatever they wished for.

Beauty is clear in the instant;
weakness or strength, in season.
There is no time here to remember
patience, patience.

Or to turn, or to think of turning
from your years at the window,
gazing deeply into this letter
you have received, or written.

HOW IT ENDS

Wind and a weakness, dandelion
letting go
through a rift in summer. Someone imagines
loving the cold.
Out of the clouds the slant wish,
one color—
dust on the pond, your breath
closing a mirror.

II

SHORT CUTS

SIGNS, SIGNS!

That summer, phenomenal creatures.
I struck a match: white-eyed,
a rat surged in the john.
A fan of wings,
staticky, strobe-clear,
rippled my brow and was gone.
That summer of blackouts and thunder
I glanced up. Quick
on the glass, two catbirds
joined like spills. It was dark,
it was late: my book
swam and I turned the page.
Signs, signs! Was it death, was it love
accelerating past,
near miss, or someone else's?
Or, after all, no secret,
but life, so long in the hearing—
like a stunning, thunderous
train you've stopped for,
lifelong, at a crossing.

THE GIVEN

Empty your bookbag, empty your pockets.
How will you live
with just those objects, stranded?
At school we played it:
jeans unraveling
blue, fading
miles of line,
I'd snare, with a watchspring,
shoals of cloud.
My keys ripsawed, my glasses burned.
With a whisper
I could cleave brack from water.
I could blend gunpowder
from dung and stone,
and blow you up in a scratch
improvisation of a day.
But how do we live now,
given the right tools
and the instructions—
when long, at last,
is long, and done,
done? Given a weapon
with a full clip, given love?

THE MIND-BODY PROBLEM

A blast-off, a butte, a downpour,
preposterous, of chains and afghans,
this woman, in her great unlikening,
avows it: that the body is a house.

Swayed, tinkling at some turn of thought,
like a chandelier under a dance floor,
grotesquerie so clear
there is no mistaking it for her,

she has it right: fail, be hated, die.
I have wanted to be her, saying
I am a shrine, I am a bad restaurant,
I am final under the disastrous sky.

LOCUSTS

The day the locust flew in my ear
I lay down in the circle I had mowed
and slept through sunset. Seventeen years
all my dream out in the wind
was their whisper *ignition ignition.*
How can I tell, now, pressing a finger
to lip, frost, combustible rose,
what will burn or flourish,
when they rise, shattering the streets, and sing
in the heatwave all *delay delay,*
the shrill, unbearable, of listening?

MY MISTAKE

It seems I misspoke, once, an entire roof,
shaded or lit, and unevenly littered
according to the sweep of a slender-needled pine,
and moored by one black wire to a clump of woods
and thence to everything else. I thought it was mine,
and remembered a torrent of birds there
in a morning so early it could have been the first.
But maybe it was the window, heavily in sway,
out of your parents', out of your sisters' way,
you had told me of that I was looking through.
Way up, you could make out a future
in which you would tell someone, as now I realize
you tried to, how the sun fed in the shingles,
all day, that near and nearer beast of heat
you slept against, breathless, all your last summer.
Until you packed softly, as if for one night,
and were gone forever. It amazes me.
But I who decide nothing am too often amazed,
and I should have known that window,
so vividly half sky, half slate,
was yours: since all I have left are these paler things
no one else calls love. Pardon, my mistake.

CAT AMONG STONES

Little more, but that paths contrive
dangerously to slide and how,
with softness of tread, it can draw their urge
through the lash-thin channel of its spine
in a counterflick of the tail, dissipating,
it knows. In a field, erratic in deliberation,
it tends along an isotherm,
or skirts, exactly, the lake of an odor,
as if openness itself were tortuous,
desire impassable. If it stepped across your back
you would deepen, limbless as a pond,
and go dark, all your thought
a match flame at the end of a hall,
wavering, stretched, righting itself.

HENRY

He was eighty-odd and owed nobody a cent
he would have told you. What got into his head
was the worst blizzard of the century,
when the roads wandered, and also the graves.
Field after field in memory whitening,
cell after cell, brim-full, letting go,
he launched his weak car, suddenly sure
they were living, his mother and sister,
and what, for decades, he had meant to say.
Whose was the wind, hearing and wild,
that battered a thousand mile front,
though you could hardly hear *white* hushing *white,*
hardly with your ear to the ground the hushing
O you needn't, it was nothing, really, nothing.

POST-ROMANTIC

Now that it's over
between me and Nature
I like her better.
We've given up
senseless fear,
useless hope.
She's got herself together.

Just hanging on, but trim,
surprising, capable,
she shows, toward evening,
some of the old flashes.
If her solitudes,
amazed and kind,
can't be mine,
or her gaze of waters
stirs others,
no harm done.
She's on her own.

And don't misunderstand:
it's not yearning,
but the old courtesy
of life for life,
when sometimes, often,
out for nothing,
I stop for a minute
to hear our songs
high up, crossing.

THE PITCH

Forget love, poetry.
No, my skills
are *to quip, to be second,*
to catch anything thrown.

When nothing was left but knowing,
I paced off sixty feet from a birch—
and struck it with eleven stones,
waist-high and fast. The twelfth, still going

through the dry woods with a faint racket,
like deer on the move, or a straining chair,
or the sun trying the lowest branches
as I walk the ridge, is all my waiting.

Exactly a year. Or two.
I swivel, snaring in my pocket
dawn. That was my life.
To lie and make the lie true.

SAND

True enough: you will sell all you have
for what should have been a heaven,
and deep in the feast year, as the story goes,
take the coat older than need
and, downcast behind your shades, go down to live
where there's sand in the streets all year.
Sand ends your bite, you breathe harsh glittering
as if the sky eroded, or something
in the blazing cars or invisible populace
had been beaten abstract by the sun
(your eyes rage, your every crease glares).
But it's just that the sweepers don't come
where the tracks, among warehouses, kill and free.
You shall be downcast, you shall cast yourself down
in the very poverty of your conclusions
four seasons. And ever after, as the story goes,
you shall look up, when your love is raw,
into some idea of the primordial sea
working above, mile after pale mile,
and hear, hardening the pause, the grit
in the glass, the stopped watch, the loud floor.

MEN IN TUXES

To be torsos, someone's ancestors,
ourselves in black and white
with our little, cold glasses
of *clarity clarity* raised chest high,
livers adipose, breath held tight . . .
When the fast shutter catches, between faces,
slack agony or ambushed willingness,
it's a bad shot, of course.
When in the flash our eyes,
like those the headlights stun on the road,
are consumed, expressionless, with red,
and the shapeshifting of the flames revolves
leopard, wife, mountain, furious crowd . . .
there is not water enough in the world.
We smile as we can. We let us burn.

LAST AUTUMN

In this low-angled light, the surface cooling
almost to October, you can see them waver
in the clear, upper foot of water,
swimming upstream at the exact speed of the current,
headwayless, all fingerlings.
And though I do not believe in such lessons,
how can I watch their wild, wild waiting and not cry
against all I have endured uselessly
head-on, mouth open, lidless eyes?

IN OUR ELEMENTS

1 *Water*

There in unconscious obedience,
barely together, the hurrying water.
What does it murmur? Just in passing
that you listen as carefully, thoughtlessly
as if you were listening to yourself.
Though it has no secrets, cannot be betrayed,
will not help you live, is faithless and clear.

2 *Air*

And sometimes coming down
from having too much my own way
I see desire, whitening,
torn from the grove, or a hawk
deliberate the wide stair of heat,
and know angels envy us
the gross, the raw air:

in dustless, leafless heaven,
dust would plummet and the leaves be still
but for the Will. *In your dream,
choose freedom,* they would say, *in your life,
faithful resistance.*

On the dark skyfloor, swaying,
we seem full of grace,
a lifetime hardly moving,
and what we would die for, everywhere.

3   *Water Speaks, in Envy of Earth*

That earth's is the true flowing,
at red heat, millennial in mood,
I must say at once, or forget.
Who can tell desire from motion,
or motion, ceaseless, from indifference?
Let me be cliffed and faulted,
let me be cavernous and old,
since to be wounded is to hold.

4   *Fire Speaks*

I have no time for your *heats,*
whether ardor or anger.
I abide no metaphors.
Is it love you want
or to be satisfied,
or to be happiest: betrayed, free.
I am not desire; if you pray
I will burn through your clasped hands,
through the roof, the blue,
the black and blacker,
through one last word and another,
to the nothing that our life
isn't and is and isn't.
I have no time. I am fire.

A PAUSE

That little brown bird visiting
one corner of the meadow, then another,
for a wrapper, a twig, some fuzz-color,
is unerring, it seems, though maybe,
the world so various, so much of it dangling,
there's not much possibility of error,
and any looping out and returning
tightens, by nature, into a nest.
What is it about wonder,
strong weakness, will to be surprised,
that where there is no home, lets us live,
and just when we forget how, flies?

ASKANCE AND STRANGELY

If there's thistledown to catch
or a petal on water,
slow hand. To coax
a lash from the eye—
slight is wary,
hard if hurried.
Shier than these,
lighter than light—
O wind punishes, wish deters—
in a century?—
no, not one shall be mine.

A MEASURE

Now that my hands are full, the world, anyway, on the fly,
and there is not time enough even to know what I know,
I take the heft of things by eye.
How many stones to that willow, how much lightning in the jay,
the drag of the jay's blue shadow across the lawn,
strict at noon, but something else at evening,
something over us like a second evening,
I can tell without stopping to lift.
I can tell from the taut soft inward of your arm
which of your fingers, driving, rests straight on the shift,
or which, consensual, is last to uncurl.
I weigh, at a distance, all of our comings together
in the story told, or lighter, untold,
on the one hand, as they say, or on the other.

III

CHILDREN'S CHILDREN

OUT OF SCHOOL

In our narrow strip of wild, at any season,
though early spring, when you've begun to notice
the hard-leafed grasses and low myrtles
that have been green all winter, is when they're likely:
two girls on horses, with so much bobbing and digression
around what wind has downed or rain deepened
that you have to slow, yourself, to be sure of their heading.
It's a first love, I'm told, something like boys with dogs,
shier, though, more determined—with so strong a privacy
I can hardly show, meeting them, such broad friendliness
as between strangers on a March path,
and far from town, is endurable.
If it's sexual, as they say, how huge the obliquity.
Those outsize eyes. I can't tell: crazed, kind?
The dark, deadbolted mountain of a body.
Does a man look that way? I suppose I do,
and yet in a tale or dream, the breathing house
everyone else walks into, but that you, weakly at the door,
thunderous, soundless, fail at entering
would be your own body, wouldn't it, that, the next morning,
hopeful, or mildly resigned, and half-forgetful,
you might feed, cluck softly to, take for a jog?
Your riding on unutterable—something—
between seasons, on no path at all, near dawn,
with a friend who may or may not stay a friend?
It is the thing to do forever, I want to tell them,
meaning *I have learned nothing all these years, nothing.*
Which is true for an instant as I stumble
through the sudden give (snow yielding) of a white door
into a morning dense, like a house shut up for winter,
with leaf odor not yet coalesced as leaves:
into my life again, inviolate, unwished for.
But *nothing* is something. I could tell them—
since they think it's revelations they are waiting for—
how many of them time never will reveal.
If we diverge, with only a nod, towards what is coming,

only my silence meaning, if it can,
the world is as much yours now as it ever will be,
well, no one young could believe it—
though with our distance widened to a shout,
wavering again, I wouldn't mind stopping to hear
any voice, even my own, whisper that spring
is again unthinkable, again mysteriously clear.

EARLY VIOLETS

Because they were the first of the year,
we stopped to give what was due
to their concentration of violet
from humus and vast air.

Desire that pure could wither you,
rage strike you to your knees.
In our first year we stepped among them
unshaken, our eyes that blue.

May the beauty you can't live without
be found with weaknesses you can live with
I wish someone had wished for me,
though, wished or not, it often happens,
and though, built father- and motherless, this place
will do just fine when blessing fails.

This land has human heft. In handy sizes,
professional buildings and convenience stores
reach further, each year, into the pockets of farms
that October turns into a faint sulfuric stew
of frost-bitten broccoli and kale
you think is your car when unexpectedly
it strikes you, out on the interstate.

It's houses that grow here, wandering rows.
Their swept lawns and fussy shrubs
could be brought indoors, yet, coming upon
this neighborhood left out all night in the wet,
you surprise something, or it surprises you
like lovers' baby talk, or a smeared dish,
as if, at whatever time, you had knocked too early,
and it opened to you in something pink and sleepy.

Indoor strangeness, outdoor intimacy—
these are my people, after all,
middle class, suburban American,
whom I must have loved, these decades, since I stay,
or loved their place, so wildly overcivilized,
I tell myself, that civilization fails.
So that, in a last and careful strip
of on-and-off brook, woodland, graveyard, park,
I can walk four miles, in a leafy season,
and, if I don't look close, see scarcely a house.
The wires miss me, I stride above the roads.
In this unlikely desert, no, in these *deserts*

tiny as the spaces between words
in a voice that has talked so long you cannot hear it,
my fellows, carp and starling, mockingbird and coon,
are trash animals, mostly, waiting for darkness,
or foraging, as this land teaches best,
with the cover of sheer obviousness.

And if I *don't* look close, it's that there's pain in seeing
how cheap the dreams are, how expensive, in a place
that has no poverty for an excuse.
And yet of all things isn't dreaming the hardest?
Others do most of it for us, and even
if elementary rage is adequate defense
against this year's bodies, or the silver digital cars
that slip, dark-windowed, under the medical center,
or that other dream *that there will be no dreams,*
well, there are the great scenes, there are the songs
that drive me out for a walk, deride me at home.

I like, after all, that this place makes no excuse.
Given a little paint, a day of mowing,
it is, sadly or happily, just what one
neighbor after another wanted it to become.
Unreal, its children say, too easily,
and year by year they do no better:
cheap dreams will dream up cheaper rebels.
My friends in the hills think they need nothing.
My friends in Manhattan think it is all there.
Who can be deceived, here, about independence?
Seeing how quiet imagination is, how word by word
unlikely, and possibly impossible,
choose, since you must choose, what cannot fool you.
We live with whom we live with, but a place
holds solitude, whatever size and shape.
It's where we don't live, and how we don't.

This place, any place, is distance,
and good enough, if only you can, to die
slowly and honestly enough to call it living.
Out on the bypass, from a little rise,
I can see the tracts on fire with watching,
a flare in the windows leaping whiter, bluer,
and feel, making my way, if feeling is ever words,
Out here without you, in your darkness,
I alone am blind. Yet I can measure
one fragrant road kill's fade to the next
until, at the merge, one newer than the rest
shames me for a second with the openness
of its weak request, its sad hunger on the air.
I will hang what I have found
in the scrub alder next to the moon
and in its raw light slowly grow unwise,
breathing in half-willingly the yaw,
the ripe cheese, the soft ammonia of death,
though it may scare off others of its kind.

SETTLERS

After a full night you will find, high in the thicket,
a tennis ball, a flat sparrow upended, and what seems
amazingly persistent snow but is a towel,
and know from their glistening that our little stream
in a soft tirade has risen and left them hanging.

Funny how when we moved here that rusty trickle,
which at normal flow a trout would scrape in,
undrinkable probably, and these acres of blackberries,
just minutes ripe when the starlings sweep them clean
convinced me we could stay here. Or was it that I loved you?

It was August, and August again, full surge,
though it was windless, of the slashing waves
we questioned, elbow-, shoulder-deep, for berries,
dogged and cross, as if it were our duty to gather
that rocky undertaste of all food, bitter and seedy.

What kept us sleepless, we said, was the eighteen-wheeler
wavering last night over the ravine,
free for a revolution, nothing that it was,
and paying who knows what as it touched the ground.
Where do things go that do not sink in?

Lips breathed open, lightly closed eyes,
you paused in a frame of thorns, and another,
each face different—stung, searching, satisfied—
but I had slackened in my picking, the first stars stranded
in a sky dark and tangled as the cores of the bushes.

In the bath your cuts, in constellations, sang,
and you raised your arm, transparent with pain
like a midnight miled with lightning, and showed me
the time-drained, flash-fixed, isolate hills
of some world without us I had been moving in.

It's a metaphor, of course, *touch*. Nearness is firmness,
the repulsion, over distance, of electron shells.
Galaxies blow through each other without collision,
though a deflection is observed, the stars drilled brighter
because they have not sufficed each other.

Take black, leave red, or, choosing at evening, blind,
choose so lightly it seems you wait to be chosen,
since it's ripeness that comes most easily to hand,
your head against the sunset, tilted as if listening,
so close they are in the mouth, sweetness and pang.

MARIGOLDS

H.M.B. 1898–1987

When you fell silent again, subsiding in your chair,
I'd tell that watchman behind your eyes our story:
how you instructed me in love of a garden,
and how, though landless in an apartment,
I scatter in harsh soil near the foundation
and on the bank that floods flash clean
our illicit and unstoppable marigolds
that flourish forgotten, hardly minding
if a dog or volley of children flattens them.
You might peer broadly, hearing that,
as into a dark room from somewhere brighter,
and begin again: *You used to follow me*
with your little wheelbarrow. But the petunias . . .
I don't remember the petunias . . .
Where did they wilder you, those sentences
you never found the end of, trailing off,
till I rose, unnoticed? When death knocked,
Grandfather, surely you were out walking
after a word, a blossom, and out of earshot.
I would not be startled, any evening,
to see you nodding slowly at the window
like a hoer, or a great sunflower.
You might have come off a cold trail, dazed.
You might have brought from a wet, head-high meadow
rushes and loosestrife sheaved
with petunias, say, or marigolds,
a few, like large, first drops of rain,
astray on your shoulders and hair,
having blundered, sheepishly, back to a life
you could not remember ever having left.

SONG FOR KATE

What are they doing, Kate?
They're singing.
Are they happy?
No, they're singing.

1

The windbreak thinning,
I can see, along the rise,
through knee-high stubble, antennas
or the any-colored gleam
of passing traffic:
Route five-three-five, the river
that flowed along my dreams,
I paraphrase, but joking,
since what I can least imagine,
of all things, is your speaking.

Who knows but the whine of tires
and their hiss in rain
never ending,
you may think traffic is silence,
and that high-pitched
singing of the will,
accustomed, may grow inaudible,
and be absent from all you do
and go without saying.

No—feet up, holding you,
one hour, two, of your nap,
I will be free of hope
and wish for you not even,
in sweet hypocrisy,
freedom from my sins,
as your sleep, reaching
for the bottom, steadies on it,
and I am myself the lazy
sure grip of the planet.

2

The unimpeded passage of the clouds
above us, the *weight light weight*
of cloud and sun and cloud on your closed lids,
is what you hear of my English over you,
or see of my face, if you can see that far,
and *maybe maybe not* and *maybe* in a murmur
of light or sound or pressure
is all you can learn now, all you remember.

There was a mnemonist who held faces,
whether from care or desperation,
in such infinitesimal detail
that a raised eyebrow would crack his concentration
and the passing cloud of a mood
change anyone past recognition:
god lover stranger stranger.

—Too much what I have done
through happiness perfect enough,
my beauty memory, my desire loss:
always the thought
I could take this with me meaning it is gone.

Watching myself from above
not shoplift at a convenience store,
startled or furtive
or hamming for the monitor,
I am the tyranny of the eyes
over us that all speaking becomes,
and which, for a second,
the turn of a good sentence saves me from.

But for you who barely find my face,
barely hear my words,

I can reach any perfection.
I can, merely by wanting to,
be all the good of the world
for you, in your buzzing drowse
so like me, so like my father,
that I could love all of us.

Now as my lullaby descends in you,
for years and for years,
waters pull it apart.
Car is *doorway* and *house* is *hours*
and the face moving an instant over the waters
and the hand breaking through
are all life saying nothing,
night after night almost nothing—
dark, night and day, and the fall
of a fine calciferous rain
houselessly through the darkness
that builds up, like a reef,
the deep white of the brain.

3

Suddenly you are three forever,
and your childish-wise
loving and speaking leaves your father
every day happier, more broken-hearted.

I understand, now, how the gods
loved us beyond endurance
with a love so vast and helpless
they kept half to themselves,
because we would crumble at their touch,
and they, so little we knew
of them or their purposes,

suffered equally from our bitterness
and our gratitude.

And what we thought was betrayal
was their last gift, to vanish,
and move among us, mortal.
Embraces muffed, simplicity archaic,
they watch in shirtsleeves from their benches
our rage at nothing they were,
old bachelors, now, or awkward parents.

Their ferocity of love, I will keep it,
since there is no way to say it,
nothing it would not batter.
When you look, years from now,
you will see an old man raging at matter,
nagging at lines.
I will be gone. I will be everywhere.

4

What good is this song
now we can talk?
Into your babbling stream
gratefully I release
some disabling dream
of mastery or immortality
I caught when I was young.

Now I have come to an end,
I murmur as before *you you,*
but mean just you, just me
and the unbroken
circle of our listening,
nothing to pray for or expect,
no one to dazzle or attract.

I cannot fear, with you in my arms,
a night noise I might fear alone,
but say it is the frost
feathering the hill
or stars grazing the roof—
a story children might believe or tell
and, forgetting who has told it,
believe myself.

This song, though useless now,
I leave where it may be found,
because at thirty-odd
with a child of your own,
having risen into a god,
you will find yourself helpless
before love, and wonder
if all you feel was felt for you.
It will be yours, at last,
in a quiet hour like this,
when you wonder, as I wonder now,
how you became forgiveness.

AT FIRST, AT LAST

In this later season I find it good:
whatever cooled, and crazed in cooling.
Brightness of fracturing rivers.
That street, who would have thought it had a name?
That speech, in ruins, that we thought we understood.

There are strangers, now, where there was no one,
poignant and small.
Even the body, white frond,
is lunar and translucent, cool.

I could stop anyone in the street, invincible,
my failure a perfect disguise,
to invoke, as their myth would, the first fire
no memory touches, that would bear no eye,
though they walk on it, breathe it, think it imaginable.

*

In that country, the guest was welcomed heartily
who might be a god, and most heartily
in the green underwater light before a storm
when skirts crackle, lifting, and the yard dog mutters.
It is said: steady, meeting those sea-gray eyes,
lest they become the sea. And how, seated at their table,
strangers, also to each other, could we look away
though apples blued above us in the evening,
though we found ourselves in the open,
our hands bark, and fragrant
in the first coaxing of the rain?

*

As any antic in pajamas
and a helmet thinks he is doing,

locked in terrible argument with a city
as large as this one, touching it nowhere.

     ★

Hunger so pale it cannot be appeased,
they are clasped asleep in heartwood, or on the brink
of waking, forever, in inaudible thunder,
their heads stone. So the stories go,
of reward, of warning.

As if their day had slowed,
and slowing, they fell
as the drowsy sinking in of rain,
their eyes relinquished

into the wall of a lily, gaze in the round,
its bell. *To see* was at last *to hold.*
To hold within: the closing of an eye.
To die—
another intimacy we could not endure.

     ★

No, it is we who are the dead
and fallen, though we think we would remember
our life as the air: to be flown through, to be sung into.
When we were each other, and did not need to rage

against the where of words, and all rage spent,
murmur silly pale elegies
for love, like the blind child at the bus stop, face upturned
for the warmth, just for the warmth.

     ★

Had initial conditions varied
by as little as one percent
no stars would have formed,
or the stars would have stormed out
light, hot elements, no carbon,
no one to sing *On and on.*

A quantum fluctuation
in the first nanosecond,
your bronze home would require
no augury, your door
open on the sun's core.

If critical constants had altered
by your early consent, unaware,
granitic shores would evaporate
at sunrise and the lake,
one level blue
cirrus, drift from its bed.

A billion universes
too hostile for us;
this one is as it is—
Anthropic Principle—
because we survive to observe it.
Who can imagine a change small enough
to make love possible?

    ★

That they throve with the simplicity of fiction,
those ancients, is their mystery.
That desire struck one head on,
so he took to his bed, that it departed
as in the garden dawn
departs from a stone. That he could say,

unjudged, unjudging, in the end,
as if no life were his to be taken,
having had beauty is what I have.

Now he is dead, let those others grieve.
Bring, in particular, her who, when he drank,
felt his underlip spread on the cup,
and knew the few mouthfuls, rolled around,
that coated his entire inner surface.

Because she will not be thinking of herself dead.
Nor will she attempt consolation,
since desire is inconsolable
and humble, seeing nothing of itself.
Whereas to praise wisdom is to seem wise.

★

And isn't it love, too, that wish,
each generation's, to be beyond love.

And if it fails, no one can change.
Pain builds nothing. Love is: just to be loved.

What's a story, anyway, but desire beguiled?
I'm not a kid. I don't expect to be satisfied.

Yet once I braked, downshifted, and we bowed
an instant in the same direction.

Yet once you hauled yourself from the water
and, still flowing, touched my shoulder.

★

Never for me, archaic elegy.
Passion dispelling
passionate disappearance
is our way:
of memory.

Because of my restlessness, I understand nothing.

I understand:
comfort as illusion
illusion as temporary
temporariness as permanent
permanence as comfort.

I choose my opposite for praise: patience.

If you fire a rifle straight up, at the apex,
all violence returned to potential,
you could catch the bullet between your lips.
I think of the other bullet resting
an instant on his unbruised brow.

As if to be patient were to lose nothing.

　　　*

Someone you took for sunset is out burning,
letters maybe, in the carless lot.
Gestures large, already memory,
he stirs brief flares from a wire basket.
All he believed in will be gone
except belief, the aroma sour rose, rose horizon.
And the twilight warms with it, turning to you
with the confession, too soon,
I am much, I am so much like you.
Autumn, evening, inhalation of ghosts:

these are the lines everyone weeps over.
What a relief, our fraudulence. How real it is!
Someone has taken weariness for renunciation,
there, out late with a fire, looking for darkness.
Someone, anyone, the leaves over your shoes
in rivers, irreparable blossom.

★

In the wintry twilight, rounding a corner,
you are already too close when you see them,
one harder, one softer,
though you can't tell, really, which is the victim.
All is, experience counsels, *for the best,*
but the watering of your eyes is automatic
as if something else assumed all separation tragic.

Well, they are young excuses—them or you?
This is a school that is never out of session
whether or not you have anything to lose,
and is endured, at any age, innocently and alone,
joy and shame and heartbreak, concluding nothing,
since you can't tell, since you may never know
whether love or freedom is the lesson.

★

If they were like me, having made all things
deathly beautiful, they left,
needing all time alone
to forgive themselves what they had done.

They are like you, taking my delighted
bending over our child as praise:
she is your child.

But if I am bitter at our life,
you are contemptuous,
having borne greater wrongs secretly,
since divine bitterness, solvent of planets,
would be fatal, even to the god.

★

On satellite infrared, false-color,
it might appear as violet, the disturbance
spreading north . . .
They are the swerveless, the slow-feeling
currents and ranges,
their vengeance, beautiful and exact,
suffering dispersion
over a whole coast, in the twelfth generation.
I feel it as spring, their accidental
exaltation or blame,
or as justice, I
who can deserve anything.

★

I have sworn never to say again
how the round-leafed plant the window dazzles
into seven huge greens
fills me with stupid happiness.
Because to dally without you
in all that precious trash of the moment
is to toy with death, or a weak
dream of it that I can bear, and worse,
to dangle before you as a grace
mere circumstance, when everywhere
lives are eaten out with famished watching.

What should I fill your eyes with but that gaze,
ungrasping, panoramic,
with which the shoals of dead face the night
for, as we are told, our power to the good
needs us poor, needs us light and free.

Or maybe not, or maybe because
I am weak and forget, or arrogant:
one more time
the songs dusting us from the fast cars all summer,
those old new songs,
sing me. *No one has said, has ever seen,
no one has ever loved like this*
go the songs of innocence. And I believe.

★

And if it is a faith you can afford,
allow me, for my services, this one word *lilac,*
and agree to know exactly what I mean

by standing eye-deep in its odor, by the cringe
from groin to panged tongue,
as if some shame you can't remember struggled out
the same door in every cell
impossible beauty was trying to get in.

As if the sea were lilacs,
combers of them, rustling cones.
Sootheless now as spring, their animal restlessness.
Almost passion, their rush among the pilings.

★

Their terrible austerity quaint now,
the silence at their tombs, melodramatic,
alas, alas, the gods are strictly poetic.
And who can revere their slangy progeny
in Deco temples of the Thirties
like unto refrigerators,
or glass-curtained Manhattan,
less awful than my stereo, my laptop?
I hear of brilliant heartlessness
and sex as uninflected and free
as the black-lined glint of vapor lamps
at midnight on the continental parking lot.
I think I already know how to desire
its gods, their vertical pupils, silver hair,
and the night they deal, so ravishing and corrosive
even the skyline will not return.
But I know what will happen to them,
alas, and I cannot worship anymore
because the gods, the gods have grown too young.

     ★

How fragile, Sunday on the avenue,
as if some desperation had been removed, some protection.
All the couples just up are carrying bakery bags
slowly, elbows in, hearing out wide.
And the amazed geezers piloting their cars,
larger somehow, windblown.

     ★

And when the rains had hardly slackened
fires broke out, and everywhere on the hills
your gaze lit, yes, the blur of heat,
and a cardinal of flame, alarm.

In the global warming: your hair pulled tight,
kerchiefed, unclean,
your lips dark and slick, your blouse
translucent, sinking in *can you want this?*
No one can lift this.

In the fever *can you want this*
the street, in suffering twilight, pooled
in our black drive, the dandelions
gone to frail puff, lifting
in a long tongue through the chainlink, tin-tinning.

And to be free, you decided you would never sleep,
and the second night *can you want this*
the light staying on in your brain
showed you busy, quiet reefs,
bruise-like anemones, gingerly currents

of the ocean in the fever
rising, feeling our rooms.
And you woke to look,
and found no difference waking,
no mystery, nothing clear,
desire nothing held
and a match hiss *yes*

★

This too shall pass they say
you can say anyway.

And yet the opposite is also true
will often do.

What goes up vanishes.
Things fall of their own weightlessness.

Therefore we bless our errors,
true to us forever.

Who loves his disease,
to be cured must be cured of love.

Yet even to say *I believe nothing*
how much you have to believe.

    ★

The ingenuity of our kindness, first,
the heat of the pillows,
and the reminder I left folded on your desk
will become unreadable.
O, as early as tomorrow,
all memory overwritten
of the forty years it took us to get here,
and only half-here—bitter, relieved, regretful
—they will say a single wave, transcontinental,
dropped us walking distance from where we are,
the site of the house uncertain; our burial, simple,
without household implements, and far from water.

    ★

And why, since even the air
buries them, or the eye's transparency,
and they can touch nothing as themselves,
but, grotesque in need, bear on us
as swan, canyon, runnel of gold—
why should they not be given in compensation
silly powers: stone-breaking glances, the choosing of winds?
They who, knowing to the end, can wish for nothing,
would wish if they could

that we did not think we believed in them,
or that we could not, in our ignorance, compose
stories so like their knowledge, weightless:
Once upon a time. The end.

★

Fame I could wait for.
Money I worried about but did not love.
Love I had and hadn't
according, I thought, to my will.
Which was the God, then,
I honored with obsession,
until, worn smooth
and joyless by the repetition,
I remember nothing
except again and again
trying to write out, just once, his name?

And when from its weakness
or my strength
language disobeys,
and every word
two sentences
speaks or speak,
and I can say nothing,
I come again,
tireder now, wanting nothing,
to a place I can hear,
as I heard when younger,
next year next year?

★

Never, or in another country, the ending:
whoever would have been its author,
a mere character by then, and ignorant,
remembers *they were in another story*
and our patience with beginnings,
as it must, begins.

★

I am younger than my friends
and their children
and their children's children
I wrote and unwrote when I was twenty,
not sure what it meant.
Thought I can neither enter nor forget,
a room you might be sleeping in.

FOR THE CHILDREN

Sometimes like a chill from the front page
freshly brought in, or leaning deeper
into the TV haze, just before spring,
they catch it, and pull their beds around them.
Or in the quick resistless eye to eye,
invisible breaker down the halls at school
lifting fliers, as they are drawing
the one breath that must last all their lives,
they cannot keep their feet, and are drowned
heavily, heavily. Drowned even in the land,
its weight of rain and roads,
and time that is so heavy.
                              Neither to leave nor stay,
not to be other than this, forever?

It will be spring, tell them. Tell them,
if you can, this is a mood, a day, a word.
You: who thought you would live forever or die
on and on. You, so happy now just to have lived,
bought, arranged, postponed,
that you cannot let yourself fear envy love hate them.

You do not go with them doing it,
one or two or even four in a car,
bodies like filling curtains,
blue rising up their thighs, under their nails,
though it is for you, too, this warm blue snow
builds on the windshield. For you somehow,
you the unimaginable, you worse than death.
Look up with them, from so far down
in yourself that you look up to the moon
as if it were your own white pupil
you could not climb to look out of, and it is closing,
and down where you are, your looking at it is closing too.
                              Freedom from fear
do they want, from hope, freedom from freedom

is it? No, they are dreadful to us,
their solemnity, their rage.
Such faith: to believe in their pain,
to take it at its word, *forever.*

It is just a word, say. Say you have kept working,
have mastered life, feel nothing. Say they are young,
or you are tired. *I am tired.*
I am so *weary* with where they are going
I cannot stand to hear the words still true to them,
dying of love, deep as the sea, spring-sick,
stoned out of my mind, wasted, despairing.

Who can remember, who can follow them,
quiet as prey, holding each other, as if their speed
into the sky, blue snow, tearing at their hair,
as if acceleration, thrusting them back, leaning them
around a corner, could hold them together,
or that sleep, in the blueing, rich garage.

Wendy and Allison, Steve and Jimmy,
that you were weak and cruel on your drug or your heavy love,
that you tore yourself with mirror-flaunting,
pendulous for beating, slender for desire,
that you lied titanically, not knowing you were trying to be true,
and in the spring, the spring that swung you by the brain,
you were not half yourself,
sick and exhausted, sweaty and sex-sore,
with that reek of giddiness and Marlboro in your hair,
trivial, sly, contemptuous, greedy and vain,
and your rage, if you knew it was rage,
scattered you, that you believed everything,
and in your great faith threw it away
—how can this matter to a father? I would lift you out,

but habit has made me faithless, daily timid insurance.
Rain, not likely today. Death not likely.
Unbearable loss, not likely (or I shall change,
O faithlessly, into the one who would give up anything,
bear anything, just to have gone on).
Heretofore unknown, naked, mountainous humiliation:
not likely. All of it certain!
Pity me that I can look on you and not die for pity,
that I am nothing you can believe
when you ask *why should I live?* and I say *having been.*
I would lift you out, blue and faint,
if I believed, if I could only remember.
You who believe the wind and are blown,
you who believe even in words and say yourselves away.
You whom a word shatters, lying on the wind,
light as rain falling, as windy rain, rising.

ELEGY FOR EITHER OF US

for John

Just when I think it's over, in a half-hearted motel:
the curtain tucked up in the rod so you could see,
the matchbook left by the bed, one missing, our signal.
As if days were rooms we stayed in for a day,
and this is a day you used phantasmally
in the life that startles mine at oblique angles:
sunlight draining from a landing,
a boy so like you I am glad and kind.
How can I tell these transits from imagination,
memory, whatever is telling me all this?
In September, of course, that door you left open,
I dreamed a garage, a whole wall of tools.
Yours, I thought, *autumn, and to fall,*
and that I should not try to say more.
Wind quiet, words quiet enough, you can drift nearer.
I remember—we wouldn't have said this to each other—
how we thought, as we aged, our feelings would grow mild.
Once, it is true, I waived every blessing,
thinking, rightly or wrongly, if I had nothing
all that belonged to no one would be mine.
But I grow rich against my will. Twenty years later,
you are not my brother any longer, but a child,
not my death, but my daughters':
I do not fear it; I hate it,
not as fate any more, but injustice,
the one word stuck forever in the throat.

AS IF ENDING

Because Kate stood, face pushed to the screen,
cheering *fuck off, fuck off*
into the swim of summer,
I don't know what, but *because*
opening day-wide into the milling of crows,
and what will come later, their comical rage . . .
Even, today, the tactfulness of death,
how it delays so long we can believe anything:
we are dead already, we are immortal,
that the sight of our child, or only
all this guessing brings it on.
Everywhere, this season, I remember
a couple at a railing, leaning out.
What they are saying I can never hear, but it means
it is impossible to stay together,
and since that changes everything, they stay.
How can they be us—they have only just met,
remember nothing, do not know what they are doing,
think, wonderingly, of their lives
grace not ours, violence not ours.
As if they too had been there yesterday,
when a migration little different from evening,
leveling, took its long place on the water,
ending nothing, since nothing ends.